THERE'S NO PLACE LIKE HOME

MARC BROWN

Parents Magazine Press • New York

Library of Congress Cataloging in Publication Data
Brown, Marc Tolon.
   There's no place like home.
   Summary: Describes in verse the many kinds of homes—
holes for worms, swamps for crocodiles, or a cat for fleas.
   [1. Dwellings—Fiction. 2. Stories in rhyme] I. Title.
PZ8.3.B8147Th 1984 [E]   84–4229
ISBN 0–8193–1125–1

5975

To Laurie,
who makes our home
so wonderful

Long ago when
Dinosaurs roamed,
The family cave
Was home sweet home.

Now there are houses,
Fancy and plain,

To keep warm in the winter,
And dry in the rain.

Homes in the city
Are steel and glass.

Homes in the jungle
Are bamboo and grass.

You can live in a house
That's pink or white.

Or by the sea to guide
Ships through the night.

Would you like to live
In a mobile home?

Just step on the gas
When you're ready to roam.

If you live in a tent,
You can save on rent.

If you live in a boat,
You're always afloat.

Some like spooky homes.

Others like kooky homes.

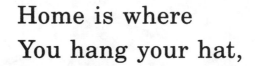

Home is where
You hang your hat,

Or where *you* hang
If you're a bat.

If you were a bird,
Would you live in a spruce,

Or build your nest
On a friendly moose?

Home is a hole
For a worm or a mole.

Pigs like a pen.
A coop's for a hen.

Some think it's swell
To live in a shell.

And fish like the motion
They find in the ocean.

A cat won't be pleased
If it's home for some fleas.

A mouse house is small
Inside of a wall.

Frogs and crocodiles
Know where to romp.
They feel at home
In a muddy swamp.

All kinds of animals
Live in a zoo.

I know an old woman
Who lived in a shoe!

Think about pet homes—
A cage, or a tank.

A bowl for guppies.
A box for puppies.

A plant likes soil.
That's where it grows.
And glasses are always
At home on a nose.

There are so many things
At home in a pocket.

A launching pad
Is home for a rocket.

So castle or dollhouse,

Teepee or dome,

Whatever it is,
There's no place like home!

About the Author

MARC BROWN is the author/illustrator
of many children's books including
WITCHES FOUR, PICKLE THINGS
and THE SILLY TAIL BOOK.

    Mr. Brown often travels around the
country visiting children at school. He
says he gets many of his book ideas
during these visits.

    Mr. Brown lives in an old house by
the sea in Hingham, Massachusetts.